MAKING THE CHANGE

This booklet relates to the report of the COSLA Working Group on corporal punishment submitted to the Secretary of State for Scotland in the autumn of 1981, and particularly to an appendix to that report in which is reproduced the last of three SCRE research reports presented to the Working Group as working papers. It aims to highlight for the general reader the issues involved in eliminating corporal punishment in schools in a satisfactory way and to serve as a manual that may guide those who seek to follow in the steps of those pioneering schools which were the subject of the research.

MAKING THE CHANGE

A study of the process of the abolition of corporal punishment

C E Cumming

T Lowe   J Tulips   C Wakeling

Hodder and Stoughton
for
The Scottish Council for Research in Education

SCRE Publication 76

ISBN 0 340 28180 4 (Cased)
    0 340 28175 8 (Limp)

Printed and bound in Great Britain for Hodder & Stoughton Educational, a division of Hodder & Stoughton Ltd, Mill Road, Dunton Green, Sevenoaks, Kent, by Lindsay & Co Ltd, 16 Orwell Terrace, Edinburgh EH11 2EU.

CONTENTS

ACKNOWLEDGMENTS

First among those who must be thanked are the headteachers, staffs and pupils of the schools which were the subject of this study. Confidentiality demands that they be anonymous.

Thanks are due also to a number of bodies; without their support the research would not have been done. The Scottish Education Department and the Education Authorities of Grampian, Lothian and Strathclyde financed the project; the three Education Authorities also released the personnel to undertake the fieldwork; the Principal and Board of Governors of Moray House College of Education, Edinburgh, seconded Dr C Cumming on a part-time basis to SCRE for the latter phase of the project.

The success of any project depends on those who actually conduct the research and it is particularly pleasant to be able to acknowledge the invaluable contribution made by the teachers and psychologists seconded by local authorities who made up the teams for the first and second phase of the project. They are identified overleaf.

Thanks are also due to all those SCRE staff who have provided stimulation, interest, and countless services to the research teams, and particularly to Mr J L Powell, Assistant Director SCRE, for his contribution to the formulation of the ideas expressed in this booklet.

Finally I wish to express SCRE's special thanks to Dr Jenny Haystead, who was in charge of the project during its early stages, and to Dr Cumming who, after taking over the project in July 1980 on Dr Haystead's resignation, carried the project to a successful end and drafted the present booklet on the basis of the earlier reports written by the reasearch teams.

W. B. Dockrell
Director, SCRE

FOREWORD

by Dr Malcolm R Green, Chairman,
COSLA Education Committee

Corporal punishment is an emotive subject. Its defenders and opponents argue constantly with one another in public, and in recent months the controversy has heightened as the European Court of Human Rights has deliberated whether a parent may legitimately refuse corporal punishment on behalf of a son or daughter at school. The facts, too, are disputed. Is corporal punishment used commonly or sparingly in schools? Has there been a decline in its use in the last two (or five, or twelve) years? For what sort of offences is it used, serious or relatively minor?

The research study, the results of which are embodied in this booklet will not provide answers to these questions, nor does it argue the case for or against the use of the strap in schools. The Working Group which commissioned it believed that the interests of Scottish education at the present time could best be served, not by retrieving familiar arguments or by compiling statistics, but by surveying what was happening in schools which had departed from the mainstream by eliminating corporal punishment. Such a survey, we hoped, would be of considerable practical assistance to teachers, schools and education authorities wishing to review their policy and practice in this matter. The Working Group is convinced that this study does indeed fulfil these hopes, and, on its behalf, I should like to express to those who produced it our grateful admiration.

Although the elimination of corporal punishment is the dominant underlying theme, there is a wider perspective to the study, which I hope will not be overlooked. All school sanctions operate within an overall management context, and the study's conclusions regarding the management of innovation deserve careful thought. The creation of an environment conducive to learning involves far more than a selection from a range of punishments.

The final report of the Working Group containing a more detailed account of the research study is being published simultaneously with this pamphlet. Nonetheless, I would commend this more discursive version to all interested in school education, in the belief that its value and relevance will extend well beyond the present limited controversy.

September 1981.

THE RESEARCH TEAM

Phase 1

Research Officers, SCRE

Dr J Haystead *until June 1980*

Dr C Cumming *from July 1980*

Teacher Observers

Mrs I Coull

Mr J Doherty

Mr A Grant

Mr J Hutchison

Mr J Jackson

Mr C Wakeling

Phase 2

Research Officer, SCRE

Dr C Cumming

Research Associates

Mr T Lowe

Dr J Tulips

Mr C Wakeling

INTRODUCTION

How the Research was done

In February 1979 the Secretary of State for Scotland asked The Convention of Scottish Local Authorities (COSLA) to consider the position of corporal punishment in schools. The remit of the COSLA Working Group on Corporal Punishment was as follows:

"Taking into consideration the accountability of the education service to pupils, parents, local authorities and society in general, and its responsibility towards all those employed in the service, to review the progress made to eliminate corporal punishment in schools, and to recommend action to abolish eventually such punishment, including testing by experiment in selected schools, the practical implications of alternative sanctions."

The Working Group, formed from a wide section of those informed on Scottish education, identified two distinct elements for consideration. First, there was the legal context for any sanctions used in schools. (A report to the Secretary of State on this aspect of the Group's work was made in January 1981.) Second, there was an evaluation of those sanctions used in secondary schools. In order to inform its judgement the Group commissioned the Scottish Council for Research in Education (SCRE) to undertake and report field studies. As it turned out, it was possible to find just enough schools using a variety of alternative sanctions and to monitor these schools over a year or more. And so the "experiments" mentioned in the remit were considered by the Working Group unnecessary. The schools monitored were therefore asked to make no changes in their disciplinary policy, and those that had abolished or were in the process of abolishing corporal punishment were pursuing a policy of their own choice. In no sense were the policies of these schools set up for the benefit of the researchers; had there been no research, they would have made the same changes.

In the first and main phase of the field work (February–June 1980) a set of twelve schools was the scene for classroom observation and structured interviews with teachers and pupils. A sample of pupils also completed a questionnaire. In the second phase (February and March 1981) only five secondary schools were visited. In this phase pupils and teachers were interviewed and discussions held both with groups of teachers and with the senior staff of the schools. Also the feeder primaries of the five schools were visited and their headteachers interviewed.

The major field work in Phase 1 was undertaken by six serving teachers of long experience who were seconded temporarily to SCRE. With rare exceptions they were readily accepted into classrooms. Two were assigned to each school and each undertook, among other tasks of data collection, the shadowing of one class for an entire week and they shared the observation of all S3 classes in mathematics. The data from the Phase 1 research was analysed and presented as a series of case studies. The Working Group considered these case studies, requested a follow-up of four of the original twelve schools, and asked that one other school be added. The research team for this second phase of the research was composed of the present writer, one of the Phase 1 teacher-observers and two educational psychologists.

In Phase 1 the set of twelve schools had included three "control" schools—schools chosen as typical of Scottish secondary schools and not following any particularly novel disciplinary policy. The others were included because the Regions in which they were situated reported that they were either abandoning or had already abandoned corporal punishment or were using the strap "infrequently". (In fact five of these nine were found to be retaining corporal punishment though taking steps to reduce its frequency.) The observation in Phase 1 thus covered the spectrum from a control school, described by one of its staff as "a belting school", to a school where the strap had never been used. Phase 2 concentrated on just two non-belting schools, two where there seemed to be an aim of abandoning corporal punishment and a fifth school which abandoned corporal punishment only in August 1980, ie after the Phase 1 field work was completed.

The data from the initial research phase, the longer term concern of the principal investigator to understand the process of innovation in education, and the questions raised by the supervising Working Group each contributed to a focussing of the research in the second phase on certain key issues. Had the schools which had abandoned corporal punishment evolved alternative disciplinary procedures accepted by pupils, parents and staff? In the two schools which were moving towards abolition, what changes had occurred in teacher and pupil attitudes to corporal punishment in the year between the two phases? How far did the alternatives become stable parts of the school procedures and how far did they keep changing and why? What were the direct and other effects of abandoning corporal punishment on guidance, departmental and school management, and teacher-pupil relationships?

What the Research showed
Phase I

It is readily admitted that the presence of a researcher in a classroom is bound to distort somewhat the normal patterns of teacher and pupil behaviour. Nevertheless, the 600 hours of classroom life observed by the teacher-observers were largely familiar to them. The customs, rules, and roles of teachers and pupils that they saw were with rare exceptions clearly recognisable to them as strangers. In particular they noted that : 1) only a very few teachers were observed not to have established conditions in which learning could occur; 2) some classes, generally acknowledged in a school to be "difficult", were controlled quite successfully by some teachers; 3) in each school there was observed a range of learning climates.*

It seems also that, irrespective of whether a school employed corporal punishment, there was a distinct gap between the best and the worst classroom climates. In the schools which had given up corporal punishment wholly or substantially, teaching and learning went on as elsewhere. Standards of behaviour were not generally giving more cause for concern to teachers, parents or pupils than in other schools. Nor did the teacher-observers find the behaviour of pupils in the classrooms as detectably different from elsewhere.

There seemed to be one factor held in common by the four schools which had abandoned or were abandoning corporal punishment. Each school had a headteacher skilled in managing change.

Phase 2

The second phase established that none of the five schools, once having abandoned or moved towards abandoning corporal punishment, had considered re-introducing corporal punishment. The majority of opinion among staff and pupils was that standards of behaviour were no worse since abolition or reduction of corporal punishment had occurred.

While the main part of this booklet deals with the detailed findings of Phase 2, it is right to highlight here two points. First, *how* schools go about planning the change in the practice of corporal punishment is worth as much thought as *what* is eventually put in its place. Second, the alternatives with which the schools have operated are not unfamiliar to informed teachers, pupils and parents. No one single "alternative" exists. *However the point is that schools which have made moves towards abolition have had to plan and manage the whole context in which sanctions are used.*

So what!—Can it be done by our school?

Without doubt this is the hardest question of all those likely to be asked. It is true that, in 1979, of approximately 400 secondary departments, the Working Group could identify only six or seven which had completely abolished corporal punishment. It might be claimed that all the abolitionist schools described here are "unique" in one or more respects. And the research record could be quoted to substantiate such a claim. Alternatively, there are some mundane facts which, if read without prejudice, may suggest that the schools portrayed here are not untypical save that they are just ahead of the rest in this one respect—facts such as the teacher-observers' feelings of familiarity with the life they saw in these schools. (The group of teacher observers between them had an aggregate 100 years of

---

*By *learning climates* is meant the overall conditions regarding noise, activity, pupil involvement, teacher preparedness etc.

teaching experience.) Again, the fact that the abolitionist schools were not in favoured areas: only one of the schools had a real social mix, two had 100% local authority housing, two were designated as being in areas of multiple deprivation, another two had part of their catchments so described. Two of the schools had kept their "experiments" very low key so that pressures from retentionists in the community and in other schools could be kept to a minimum. One headteacher spoke of feeling isolated among his colleagues (ie, fellow headteachers). In a more general move towards abolition, support from other innovators would certainly be forthcoming. Finally, it was the impression of the Phase 2 research team that, in the two schools where corporal punishment was being phased out, the mood of staff had moved in the year's interval in the direction of recognising abolition as inevitable. Their concern was much more with the mechanics of the alternatives than with arguments over the principle of abolition. Unless the teachers in all the five schools are unusually capable in coping with change, there is some evidence that innovation in other schools could follow similar patterns. What pattern and what specific alternatives are very much for each individual school to decide. It is in this open-minded spirit that the remainder of the booklet is offered.

CHAPTER 1

SANCTIONS

Sanctions, punishments or penalties are suffered by pupils when a teacher finds the pupil's behaviour unacceptable in some way.

Sanctions are, of course, not the only means of control: positive ways of control and attempts to anticipate disciplinary situations and to avert them can also be employed. All means of control were the concern of the researchers and various positive means are reported on later in this report, but the prime focus of the research was on the sanctions that teachers employ after breaches of discipline, great or small, have already occurred.

The aims of this chapter are to describe some sanctions observed and to evaluate them. There is no intention to recommend any particular sanction or set of sanctions.

In Table 1 (p 6) there are listed some 20 sanctions observed in the 13 schools investigated in the two phases of the project. This list is arranged to reflect the degree of seriousness of the sanction—from disapproving gestures to official exclusion/expulsion from a particular school. Another way of looking at the list is to recognise that the sanctions in the upper part are used more often than those in the lower part of the list. No teacher employed all the sanctions in the list*, though it was found that teachers varied their repertoire of punishments according to age and ability level of class.

The list does not contain any novel sanctions. The majority are well known to all connected with Scottish education. It is their ordinariness which demands attention. A minority, such as 'Time Out', will perhaps be known under other labels. Only the less well known will be described here.

Sanction 7: Time Out, On Assignment, Isolation

An offender is moved from his usual class. There are two forms.

1. The pupil goes with appropriate work to another teacher who preferably is teaching non-peers of the offending pupil.
2. The pupil is left with his work in a lonely room or corridor. Supervision is likely to be by an Assistant Head and is probably intermittent.

Either form may be employed instantly when a flare-up or crisis has occurred or after arrangements have been made when it is a measure to

---

*It is to be noted that this comprehensive list was not made available to the teachers.

TABLE 1

Sanctions Employed:
A Composite List Indicating a Trend in Seriousness

1. Non-verbal cues, silences, disapproving gestures.
2. Rebukes, tellings off, to individual, group, class.
3. Lines, extra homework, punishment exercises, unproductive writing.
4. Threat of movement to other seat in class.
5. Movement of seat.
6. Threat of isolation in another class.
7. Time-out, "on-assignment", isolation.
8. Detention, unofficial, in class teacher's room.
9. Corporal punishment.
10. Threat of report, oral or in writing, to guidance or Year Head or "Office".
11. Report and possible intervention by Year Head and guidance.
12. Withdrawal of privilege.
13. Official detention, school organised.
14. Threat of parental involvement.
15. On report: behaviour timetables with or without parental knowledge.
16. Letter or telephone call to parents informing of problem.
17. Pupil sent home for clarification (a pre-suspension warning).
18. Parental involvement through visit to school.
19. Withdrawal to Special Unit.
20. Tactical or unofficial suspension.
21. Suspension, exclusion—official.

NOTE:

The order of sanctions in this table is based on the stated views of the teachers and the severity of the offences for which they said they had used the sanctions; it took cognisance also of pupils' reports of what offences particular sanctions were used for. It is to be noted that no school—and certainly no teacher—employed all the sanctions in the list.

deal with persistent misbehaviour. This "On Assignment" procedure was found to be used extensively and without procedural problems in one non-corporal punishment school. Ready co-operation between members of a department ensured that teachers would respond—with or without notice—to a request by a colleague to supervise an offender. The headteacher of this school reported some use of "On Assignment" also for offences committed outside the classroom. Three of the Phase 2 schools* used this sanction: but, only one formalised it through a pro forma.

Sanctions 8 and 13: Detention

Detention in fact crops up twice in Table 1. It has a weak version, not usually involving formal recording, and a strong version where not only will the detention be logged in a pupil's record but the senior management and guidance staff may be informed. The weak form of detention is a sanction operated by a teacher or by departmental head on behalf of a teacher. The strong version is more a school operated sanction. Supervision of detainees in the strong version is typically by assistant head teachers or volunteer promoted staff. Various kinds of work were observed being done by detainees—repetitive unproductive work, class work requiring completion or additional school work, and school maintenance work such as litter-hunting and washing school transport.

There were signs that the weak form of detention operated by class teachers was being replaced by the stronger school-organised form. Two explanations of this trend seem plausible. First, teachers who are having discipline problems in class may continue to suffer the problems during detentions they themselves supervise. Second, pupils are sometimes given detentions by several different class teachers. (For the problem pupil, the problem becomes one of finding a free time in a crowded diary!). There seem to be two real advantages to school-organised detention. To begin with, useful information on a pupil's school-wide behaviour can be collated. Secondly, when detention is treated as a more serious penalty its use becomes less frequent. The burden of supervising detention is also reduced—both by centralisation and by reduction in a number of cases—to a level where senior and/or volunteer staff are called on to undertake it only on a few occasions per year. Of course, an implication of using detention as a more serious sanction is that other lower-level sanctions have to be employed for lesser offences.

Four of the Phase 2 schools operated forms of detention. One of these schools used lunchtime detention for, since official transport was used by pupils to return home, detention after school hours would have presented difficulties. The other three schools detain a pupil after the

---

*See pp 2–3 for explanation of the phases of the project.

end of the pupil's day. These latter schools arranged to inform parents at least 24 hours in advance if a detention was to extend beyond 4 pm.

In none of the schools using detention were the staff who supervised detention rewarded. Head teachers reported that they relied on teachers taking an extended view of their professional role. One school used volunteer supervisors only; another used a rota of senior promoted staff.

Sanction 11: Reports

It will come as a surprise to many teachers that the key element in the discipline systems of three of the schools which have abolished corporal punishment wholly or partially are elaborate procedures for reporting pupils on paper. The term "paper sanctions" will be used to indicate this form of reporting. Now many, if not the majority, of Scottish secondary schools have procedures for reporting pupils to senior and/or guidance staff. However, the researchers found that, where paper sanctions are recognised by the majority of staff and pupils as being regularly and consistently used for a range of offences, they seem to acquire a currency. Moreover, the time taken for them to do so was only two or three school sessions. (The Primary 7 children of one feeder primary were certainly as aware of the paper sanction at the secondary as were the pupils in the secondary itself.) Paper sanctions have two overlapping functions: reporting action taken and referring pupils upwards for action. The reporting function is simply a formal way of passing information to guidance or senior management staff. On the other hand, a report that is completed for the purpose of referring a pupil, probably after consultation with a departmental head, constitutes an acknowledgement that a pupil has not responded to classroom sanctions. The teacher is requesting action. A member of the guidance staff or senior management team then has responsibility for the pupil. Using paper sanctions does not mean that a violent disruptive is allowed to continue while a teacher calmly writes out a report and pops it in the internal mail: the schools have procedures for immediate crisis referrals (see Chapter 2: *Crisis Referrals*).

The sequence of steps leading up to the employment of a paper sanction is commonly something like the following:

1 Warnings about behaviour.
2 Threat of report.
3 Report filled in and threat made that it will be submitted unless behaviour improves.
4 Pupil informed that the report will be submitted.

There is, therefore, no punishment event with paper sanctions. The pupil is aware of what the report contains but he never carries it to the next higher level in the referral chain. He knows that responsibility has passed to someone other than the referring teacher.

The apparent effectiveness of paper sanctions really does need examination. The research suggests that paper sanctions gain value in the following ways:

1. As individual teachers use reports with more consistency they begin to believe in the usefulness of the reports for the school as a whole.
2. Pupils note that being reported leads regularly to involvement of teachers other than the class teacher.
3. Pupils do not like one-to-one encounters with authority figures nor do they like being asked to account for their behaviour.
4. Pupils note that their parents are often informed of the guidance interview (or other event following a report). Most pupils do not like their parents to know too much of their school lives.
5. When parental interviews are held (a sanction in itself) whole files of reports may be produced: the past as well as the present is up for review.

The pupils' folklore within the school quickly incorporates the belief that paper sanctions are serious and hence to be avoided. Thus paper sanctions deter many pupils.

An additional deterrent element is consciously added in one school. Pupils and parents are made aware that reports are stored with school records and are likely to be used for example, when references to prospective employers are being prepared. (See also Chapter 2: *Permanence of Files*.)

Sanction 15: On Report, Behaviour Timetables

When a pupil is put "on report", he carries a "behaviour timetable" (a blank timetable) to every class usually for a week or two. The timetable is initialled by each teacher and an assessment of the pupil's behaviour given. (For instance, initials in red indicate unsatisfactory behaviour). Each day, immediately after school, the pupil reports to his year head or other senior authority figure. Parents can be involved by informing them in advance of the sanction being used and asking them to sign the timetable each day to indicate they know the pattern of behaviour being shown. One school reported that a few pupils asked to be "on report", ostensibly to act as an incentive to better behaviour.

Sanctions 17 and 20: Suspension other than Official Suspension

An aim implicit in those discipline systems which operate without corporal punishment is to increase the number of steps before the ultimate sanction of suspension, exclusion, or expulsion.* Schools seem genuinely reluctant to take the steps which may lead to intervention by the local authority. The research revealed two dilute forms of suspension which do not come to the local authority's attention.

---

*Official suspension/exclusion is the province of the education authority rather than the school and its operation was thus outwith the scope of the investigation.

B

In one school the sanction of being "sent home for clarification" follows a serious incident. The word suspension is not used to the pupil who is made aware of the seriousness of the offence by having to go home and return with his parents. A serious discussion is then held involving pupil, parents, and a senior member of staff, though not normally the head teacher.

Tactical or unofficial suspension is very similar to the above in intent, viz, to draw up an offender smartly. The procedure may, however, involve parents being asked to sign a guarantee of their child's future good conduct. Also, the pupil may be kept out of school for anything from an hour to four days. In two schools this sanction is used regularly with pupils who have been involved in vandalism or fighting.

Sanction 19: Withdrawal to a Special Unit

Special units within schools* are of two types. All five Phase 2 schools had a special unit. In one case the unit was used as a punishment for disruptive pupils rather than as a support to pupils. Punishment units are so different in nature and function that we describe them separately from other special units.

a) *Punishment Units*

Although not involving physical exercise or physical punishment, this sanction is the day school equivalent of the "short, sharp shock". In the school where such a unit was observed in action, no more than four pupils—and, in practice, usually one—spent the entire school day in a highly structured and supervised setting. They were clocked in and out. Breaks were arranged for them when their peers were in class. This deterrent unit quickly achieved notoriety, the majority of pupils being very keen to avoid having to go there. Re-integration, which, as will be seen, is a problem to be found in the case of the more common sanctuary type unit, was there hardly an issue at all since the maximum period in this unit was three weeks. It was standard procedure for pupils to begin re-integration by joining classes where they had caused trouble in the past. (At the time of the Phase 2 observations the scheme had been in operation for 2 years and in that time only a dozen pupils had had experience of being in the unit). It may be appropriate to consider such a punishment unit as a rather sophisticated form of "isolation".

b) *Other Special Units*

The type of special unit found in the other four Phase 2 schools, although it may be used to contain (and evaluate) pupils who otherwise would be disruptive, is not punishment-oriented. The name given by one school to a unit of this type—"The Haven"—is

---

*These units within the schools are to be distinguished from the units set up by some authorities to take seriously disturbed pupils from a number of schools. The latter are normally the responsibility of educational psychologists.

indicative of the aim of all four units—to provide alternative education for those who are not being adequately catered for in the main school. In one sense these Units are not sanctions at all. Their establishment was indeed unconnected with the elimination of corporal punishment.

Often pupils never return fully to the main stream and, indeed, are reluctant to do so. What at the outset is probably perceived by parents or pupils as a sanction becomes for many a sanctuary. The units seem particularly effective in retaining one-time persistent truants in regular attendance.* They are, however, intensive users of teaching resources since personalised learning programmes are an essential part of the education offered.

The teacher in charge of the Unit was, in all schools visited, the key person in deciding which pupils should be admitted to the Unit. However, parental involvement was also found to be the norm both in the admittance procedures and during the pupil's stay in the unit. In one school, the unit pupils were visited regularly at home by the unit teachers.

In one case there was formal assessment using tests of a pupil's academic strengths and weaknesses. For the rest, the work programme was devised on the basis of information supplied by the pupil's teachers, the unit teachers' own experience, and some trial and error. In successful units the special ethos, the skills of the staff and the time staff and pupils spend talking out difficulties do make for crucial improvements in a pupil's behaviour. A couple of problems seem, however, to be common to all "haven" units:

First, re-integration to mainstream education is a recognised difficulty. The research found that the average stay in the Units could be counted in years rather than in months. To help pupils adjust to normal schooling attempts are made to ease them back by taking them into normal classes part-time and by using in the unit some sympathetic staff from the main school to act as a link when the pupils do return. The second problem is that, to varying degrees, the education offered is restricted to the basics. Moreover, the schools do not seem to be developing curricula aimed to increase the potential for further learning for pupils who generally are under-achievers. The main problem appears to relate to designing a programme of adequate breadth, though for that additional resources are certainly required.

Sanctions: A Review and Evaluation

Pupils, of course, make their own judgements on the effectiveness of punishments in school. One would not expect their views to coincide with those of teachers and, indeed, several pupils made it clear they

---

*It is to be noted that the pupils in these units are generally of low ability. Other pupils are probably aware of this, but it must be said that their knowledge of what goes on in these units appeared to be very limited indeed. To most pupils, being sent to such a unit was probably an outcome too improbable to constitute a serious deterrent.

could distinguish their perspectives from those of teachers. For instance, one S3 boy in a school which does not use corporal punishment but does use detention remarked,

"The belt is better for us than one hour detention—but that is from our point of view . . . really from the teacher's side detention has more effect."

The sanction on which pupils interviewed were almost of one mind was parental involvement. It was, with rare exceptions, mentioned as being very effective. Some pupils made explicit reference to the fact that punishment at home is a likely result. On other sanctions there was much less agreement amongst pupils even in the same school.

We can account for the variety of views held by pupils in the following ways.

Pupils' opinions of penalties are likely to be based partly on direct experience as receivers of them, partly on their witness of the apparent effectiveness of penalties imposed on others, and partly on the communicated experience—or claimed experience—of others. (The penalties in the lower part of Table 1, such as official detention and parental involvement, are experienced at first hand by only a small proportion of pupils, and are therefore likely candidates for evaluations based on *second-hand* reports.) Moreover, pupils see the same penalty used successfully with one pupil, unsuccessfully with another; used successfully by one teacher, unsuccessfully by another. Is it surprising that their judgements vary? Indeed to ask whether a "telling-off" is effective is to equate all tellings-off by all teachers on all occasions.

A second and related point is that sanctions operate against particular offences or behaviour patterns and seek to make individuals' behaviour acceptable while at the same time having a deterrent effect on others. There is likely to be a difference in a pupil's feelings about a sanction he has suffered, and about one which he has avoided.

Finally, sanctions will have different perceived severities for different pupils and, indeed, for observers generally. This last point needs a little expansion for it is probably the key to understanding the success of the apparently very ordinary and unimpressive "alternatives" to corporal punishment. Every sanction is perceived as having a particular level of severity. Clearly, every pupil will not have the same perception: but, pupils, in their rank ordering of sanctions in terms of severity, will be reflecting the ways in which these sanctions are used in their classes or, indeed, in their school. Frequent use of a sanction and/or its use for trivial offences is likely to result in that sanction being seen as low on the scale of severity—and, by association, to be ineffective. Conversely, school-organised detention, which is usually regarded as a more severe sanction than classroom detention, tends to be the less often used—and is typically surrounded by more ceremony. The point being made is that, in a very real sense, sanctions are as severe as they are made to seem. Paper sanctions are made to appear severe through the regular action taken on them by authority figures in the school. In short, the effectiveness of a punishment and hence its deterrent value is likely to depend on its perceived severity. Thresholds differ from one pupil to another in respect of what level of severity is judged personally unacceptable. The minority who incur the severest sanction are those whom the graduated set of sanctions has failed to deter. The number in this category must be kept low and, therefore, the severest sanction must be used very seldom. Otherwise the "last resort" sanction—whatever it is—will lose its deterrent value and more pupils will behave in such a way as to require further use of that severest sanction.

This account or theory of sanctions gives support to those schools which recognise the need to put a lot of steps in the sanctions chain before the door is shown to a pupil. A discipline system which results in pupils being formally suspended before parental involvement has been tried would be likely to prove unsatisfactory—save in crisis situations—since the ultimate sanction would have been reached too soon. This theory of sanctions may also help interpret why it is that corporal punishment appears in the middle of the sanctions list whereas teachers in this research, and in other more official pronouncements, when they do support corporal punishment, claim its value to be as a last resort. Quite simply corporal punishment through common use in classrooms throughout the early years of secondary schools is just too common to have a major deterrent value. Suspension on the other hand is most uncommon at all stages: it is the real last resort just because it is used so little. The theory would also lead us to predict that over time the perceived severity of suspension would decline if schools used it as frequently as corporal punishment is currently used.

It has been the task of this first chapter to describe the substance of the alternative sanctions to corporal punishment. However, to put it boldly, the research seems to show that it is not what you do but the way that you do it. Accordingly, the following two chapters, dealing with referral systems and the role of management in discipline, describe and explain the ways and contexts in which the sanctions work.

CHAPTER 2

REFERRAL AND REPORTING

The Schools in Phases 1 and 2 of the research all had means of referring/reporting problem pupils to guidance and management staff. Generally speaking those schools which had abandoned or were abandoning corporal punishment had more carefully planned referral systems, and the systems were apparently being used. In short, the Phase 2 schools had well designed procedures which, through regular use, had credibility in the eyes of teachers, and hence of pupils. The point has already been made in the previous chapter (see *Reports,* p 8), that there is a distinction between a report and a referral. The former implies the passing (and storage/collation) of information about a pupil, while the latter is a request for help on the part of a teacher.

An Example of Innovation in Referral and Reporting Systems

What follows is an account of the referral and reporting systems of one of the Phase 2 schools as it was monitored in early 1981. The system has undergone some minor alterations since its adoption—a feature of the referral and reporting systems of all the Phase 2 schools.

Elements of a Referral and Reporting System

1   For each of the year groups in S1–S4 there is an assistant headteacher in charge. His responsibility is total for the year group. Each AHT is aided by two assistant principal teachers of guidance.
2   Teachers are expected to report direct to the AHT in charge of the year (using Form A) pupil misdemeanours and sanctions taken. (Examples of the sort of forms described in this chapter are given in Appendix C.) The AHT's role is to monitor the reports and evaluate them.
3   When a class teacher cannot control a pupil's behaviour he* is expected to refer the pupil to the head of his subject department. If his Principal Teacher does not have an effect on the pupil—say there is a repetition of the misdemeanour for which the pupil has been referred—he *refers*, on Form B, the case to the Assistant Head Teacher (AHT) in charge of the year. The AHT's role is to intervene as soon as possible. He may interview the pupil and discuss with the pupil the content of Form B and any other reports.

---

*By 'he' should be understood 'he/she', both when the reference is to a teacher and when it is to a pupil.

He *may* use one or more severe sanctions, such as school organised detention; he *may* refer upward to the Depute Headteacher.

4   As part of the work of monitoring pupils' behaviour, an AHT can use another pro forma, the Report Back form, to find out if teachers are still having problems with any pupils who have previously been brought to his notice. Whereas the information collected by Forms A and B is wholly negative, teachers can, in the Report Back form, record and forward positive information.

5   Three or four times a year teachers are asked to complete class reports. They are expected to report pupils whose behaviour is not entirely satisfactory. The aim is to spot potential problem pupils and to diagnose the problems. The role of the AHT is to interview pupils whose names appear in the lists of two or more teachers. Parents of those whose names appear three times or more may be called in. Teachers are given a confidential memorandum containing the result of the discipline survey.

Other Phase 2 schools use one pro forma to serve the reporting and referring purposes (elements 2 and 3) and use oral or less formal means to check up on a pupil's progress (element 4). The fifth element is unique to one school. Its importance may be as much in the regular involvement of all teachers in the discipline system of the school as a whole as in its explicit purpose of spotting potential problem pupils. A flow-diagram showing a typical reporting/referral system is given in Figure 1 (p 16).

Crisis Referrals

Sometimes a pupil cannot be dealt with by following the relatively slow steps of the referral system. It is a feature of all referral systems that normal routes can in some circumstances be by-passed. For instance, within the above described system, it is normal practice for a teacher—or PT (subject)—to take a pupil who is creating a pressing problem direct to the administration corridor. In one school, if available, the depute headteacher is the front man; in another school two promoted members of staff are timetabled "on call" each period to help deal with emergency situations.

Feedback

If teachers are going to spend time on paper work connected with reports and referrals, one would predict that they will want to know what happens to their completed forms, both in general and in specific instances. If they gain the impression that nothing happens, then their confidence in the discipline system—or at least the reporting and referral aspects of it—will diminish.

In Phase 1, instances were encountered where teachers' expectations that action would follow their completion of forms were not being met. In two schools, the distinction between reporting and referring had not been made sufficiently clear to teachers. As senior management staff

FIGURE 1

A TYPICAL REPORTING/REFERRAL SYSTEM

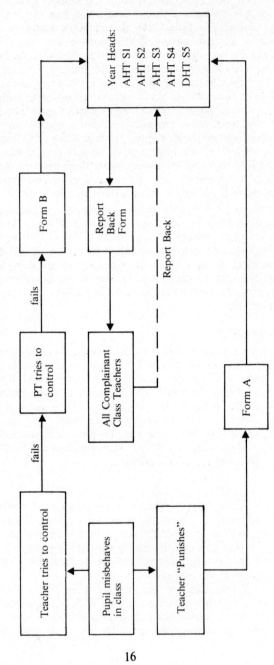

generally saw the purpose of completing a pro forma as helping them establish which pupils were at risk of being punished in several departments, feedback to specific teachers was unnecessary—or so it was argued. In one school it was held initially that where a teacher had referred a pupil upward to guidance* or senior management, the teacher's responsibility was over. (By the time of the Phase 2 investigation, a considerable amount of effort had been expended in this school in order to formalise feedback to teachers.) In one school, staff had to show, on the pro forma, whether they required feedback, and guidance staff were expected to respond using a summary pro forma. In the same school summary file-cards on pupils were available for consultation by interested staff. Generally the staff in Phase 2 schools where feedback had seemed deficient in Phase 1 were more satisfied in Phase 2.

Case conferences on individual pupils, involving all concerned staff and perhaps external agencies, were a feature of the discipline system of one school. (It is fair to point out that some of the other schools would have liked to adopt the procedure if resources had been available.) As a means of feedback and involvement of teachers in the discipline system as a whole, case conferences in this school seemed potentially very important though very time-consuming.

Monitoring of Referrals and Reports

By now it will be clear that the systems operating to collect and record teachers' views on pupils' behaviour involve a great deal of paper. Schools have had varying degrees of success in marshalling the collected data. In one school the reports/referrals were monitored initially by the headteacher, then by his deputy. In abandoning this arrangement, the school recognised that it was inappropriate for the headteacher and deputy to be involved with discipline at such an early stage. Moreover, it was clear that the burden of paper work could not be carried by the top management while the guidance staff's information about pupils was not being utilised to the full in the monitoring.

Two different series of issues arise in respect of monitoring the written reports. First, the format of the original report and the summary of it (perhaps to be kept in a separate file) need to be carefully designed. (Office/clerical staff may be used to transfer to summary files the data from the original pro formas.) The most basic summary could consist of a cross for each original pro forma on file. The second issue concerns who is to review the summaries and files and how the decisions for action are to be taken.

Mention was made in all schools of the need to allow for differing levels of tolerance of different teachers. Teachers who, for one reason or another, had not supported the system, could easily render the files

---

*See Chapter 4 for further treatment of the roles of guidance staff.

C

useless through over-, or non-, use of the reporting/referring systems. It is clearly necessary to secure the intelligent co-operation of all staff.

The research did not find the solution to these problems. There may be scope for regional or national initiatives in providing administrative consultancy services to establish systems with some of the more obvious faults removed and perhaps a degree of standardisation of forms and files.

Permanence of Files

A variety of stances were taken by schools on the issue of for how long files on pupils' behaviour should be kept. One headteacher made it clear that the reports and referrals were with pupils for their school lives and could be used for references. The currency of the reports as paper sanctions, the school held, rested partly on the recognition by pupils that the reports could be used against them. In this school parents were, however, told they could inspect the files. In another school the headteacher, in acknowledging the expressed fears of pupils, felt that the files should be destroyed each year. In another Phase 2 school there was no ostensible aim to make reports a long term threat, but some pupils were showing signs of regarding the records in this light. In two other schools the issue probably did not arise for their approaches to the use of file information were more personal than administrative.

There is here an issue which deserves wide debate and careful consideration by the public. Parents, in particular, will be concerned at the career implications of retaining records over several years. (This point is discussed further on pp 37–38.)

Openness of Recording

In comparison with the use of corporal punishment, the regular recording of misdemeanours by children and action taken, not to mention a declaration that a pupil is becoming too difficult for the teacher to control, are public acts. However, if emerging patterns of pupil behaviour are to be spotted, teachers must not try to contain the problems within the classroom. For many experienced teachers there may be resistance initially to the regular reporting or referring because, in the past, they have coped with problems on their own. For less experienced or less confident teachers there may be fears that a report will be a public admission of weakness which will blight their careers. The research found several instances of the latter fear in two schools, one of which is rapidly phasing out corporal punishment, the other of which retains corporal punishment but operates a referral system. In a couple of Phase 2 schools there were small numbers of teachers who openly did not support the reporting and referring systems. It is likely that their lack of support arose partly from the belief that they had contained, and would continue to contain, problems on their own.

Openness of recording and reporting gives rise to problems in schools using corporal punishment as well as schools not using corporal punishment. It is a task of the school management to persuade, through leadership, all the teachers to accept the school's aims and the established procedures. It is to the role of the school management in the operation of discipline that we now turn.

CHAPTER 3

THE ROLE OF MANAGEMENT
IN DISCIPLINE

Since the expansion of the number of promoted posts in secondary schools a decade or so ago, a variety of management structures have evolved. There are two levels of management recognisable in all schools, termed here senior management and departmental management. Within the former are assistant head teachers, depute head teacher(s) and head teacher. Departmental management consists of a principal teacher (subject) and, if the department is large enough, one or more assistant principal teachers. Though there will be some brief discussion of the part to be played within a department in respect of discipline, for the most part in what follows the term "management" will apply to senior management. Moreover, remarks on guidance will be kept to the minimum in this chapter since a fuller treatment is to be found in the next chapter.

The involvement of management in discipline can best be dealt with under three headings:

(i)   Management of the discipline policy and procedures.
(ii)   The contribution of curriculum planning to good discipline.
(iii)   The nature of pupil-teacher relationships.

Management of the Discipline Policy and Procedures

In all the Phase 2 schools—those which had abolished as well as those which were abolishing corporal punishment—there was found to be a clear effort to distance management staff from the initial stages of the discipline referral procedures. Four of these schools had horizontal guidance organisations which, from the pupil's standpoint, made a principal teacher (guidance) or an assistant head teacher as the normal referral and reporting point. "Above" the normal referral and reporting point there were two or three more points, viz, an assistant head teacher*, a depute head teacher, and, finally, a head teacher. Just as a sanction overused is devalued as a deterrent, too rapid a referral to a head teacher would result in the seriousness of that step being missed by some pupils. A corollary of this distancing of top management staff from routine discipline cases is that there is normally no conflict with their role in 'crisis' referrals. To explain, a pupil in a crisis situation is referred directly to an AHT or depute head teacher instead of, at least in the first instance, to his guidance teacher.

---

*In only three of these four schools.

One Phase 2 school was found to have a vertical guidance system organised in 'houses'. Each 'house' contained pupils of all ages and had three promoted guidance staff. The house system as a whole was the responsibility of one assistant head teacher. In practice, the guidance staff were the normal points of reference both for reports and for punishment (non-physical) in support of referring staff. Only the AHT (Guidance) seemed there to have regular involvement with non-crisis discipline cases. The other four assistant head teachers had some irregular involvement through being on the 'on-call' list of senior staff available in a 'crisis'.

Departmental Management and Discipline

The subject department continues to be the fundamental organisational feature of secondary schools. However, working and learning conditions vary between departments: safety and legislative consideration, for example, cause certain practical departments to have distinctive rules for pupil behaviour—and corresponding penalties for their breach.

The departmental dimension to discipline can be illustrated in the following ways. In Phase 1 it was found that forgetting equipment was regarded with varying degrees of tolerance within the same school, punishments ranging from mild reprimands to corporal punishment. It does, of course, have to be borne in mind that forgetting equipment for a practical subject is less easily remedied than it is for, say, English, where pencil and paper may be supplied with little inconvenience. Departmental rules on forgetting equipment seemed to apply. In one school with an open-plan provision the departmental head stationed himself so as to oversee problem classrooms and, on occasions, remove troublesome pupils to a central area where he could more easily keep them under supervision.

One head teacher, in formally recognising that working conditions, and thus codes of conduct, will vary between departments, stressed that departments must arrive at a code to suit their own circumstances. It is the task of senior management to ensure that departmental codes are consistent with the school's overall policy. Quite simply, if, for instance, one department allows the wearing of coats and scarfs and another does not, there is potential for confusion through inconsistency. The research showed that teachers do have somewhat different expectations of normal behaviour. While these expectations may be quite personal or even idiosyncratic (eating may be allowed but no chewing) there is some tendency for them to be standardised by departmental membership. (Teachers' allegiance to departments is often so strong that, for instance, there tends to be departmental rather than individual opposition to introducing a reporting and referral system.)

Leadership

Mention has been made of the need for senior management to ensure appropriate degrees of consistency in the operation of school discipline policy even when departments are following their own codes of conduct. Attention must be given to how the head teacher, or the head teacher and his senior management colleagues, can persuade the rest of the staff to accept and achieve the aims of the school in the area of discipline—that is how they exercise leadership.

The research revealed in some Phase 1 schools which ostensibly had discipline policies—including referral systems—that some teachers were unable to describe the policy on discipline. It was a feature of all Phase 2 schools that teachers could readily summarise the discipline system (and give comments on it). Not only did the teachers know of the policy, generally speaking they followed the procedures associated with it. It is to the substantial credit of the senior management in all the Phase 2 schools that teachers had to a great extent come to accept aims which their colleagues generally in other schools would find very hard to accept.

It was one of the additional tasks of the Phase 2 investigation to try to establish how those schools which had abolished corporal punishment, or were in the process of doing so, set about forming policies. It became clear that the policy decisions were generally taken within the management team.

While it has to be granted that all the head teachers of Phase 2 schools had strong personalities and impressed through their command of educational goals, there was no evidence that the head teachers were autocratic. Far from it, in fact. Each used his management team to hatch and try out ideas. The strong identity of the management teams and the esprit de corps which apparently existed within them may have been crucial in successful communication to the rest of the school.

It was found also that management was the initiator of policies even if the issues involved had to be open to debate by the staff as a whole. (See Chapter 5 for contrasting means of staff participation in policy-making.) A variety of means of communication were used. Staff handbooks were one instance of a means of gathering together procedural detail about reporting and referring. Two schools were found to hold frequent *ad hoc* morning interval meetings. Two others, their head teachers being convinced of the fruitlessness of whole staff meetings, operated through departmental meetings. These measures, together with such further means of communication as the issue of memoranda, individual contacts between management and staff, and link-meetings (for example, between guidance and departmental staff) were used to such effect that few teachers could have been unaware of what was going on.

Staff in all four schools reported that they were more often involved in deciding issues associated with the execution of policy than with the policy itself. Generally, the openness of management to the views of teachers was acknowledged but contrary views were sometimes expressed openly. The picture of the five schools is thus one of fairly decided managements which were at pains to consult, inform and involve the rest of the staff over means, while maintaining control over aims.

The fact that reporting and referral systems were in fact used widely probably reflects the staff confidence that had grown in the systems and in the management hierarchy. There was little evidence of teachers expressing a lack of support. The old complaint of "lack of backing" was seldom heard. The sanction of "time-out" as well as the creation of an "on-call" rota of teachers had apparently been designed by management for support of teachers and were in general recognised by teachers as being so: positive references were made to being saved from isolation in facing discipline problems.

The Contribution of Curriculum Planning to Good Discipline

The causes of misbehaviour are varied. There is reason to believe however that the curriculum can be one important source of disaffection with a school. While one head teacher may have been expressing a view shared by many educators when he said that "the curriculum cannot totally motivate", there was ample evidence in the courses of the third and fourth year pupils that Phase 2 schools were alive to the curriculum dimension of discipline. All five schools ran courses especially designed for those S3/4 pupils for whom the SCE O Grade was not appropriate. The head teacher of one school indeed recalled putting the design of appropriate courses for all his S3 and S4 pupils as the first step towards improving the discipline system. In contrast there were schools in Phase 1 where teachers up to the depute head teacher level were concerned at the lack of planned courses for non-certificate pupils.*

How then was the curriculum improved in the Phase 2 schools? The ways were, in fact, by no means uniform. One school had introduced the Certificate of Secondary Education in addition to O Grade with a view to making all pupils "certificate" pupils; another, believing even CSE options to be unsuitable for some pupils, had introduced "mini-courses" to supplement CSE and O Grade ones; another school was involved in City and Guilds Foundation courses; yet another had designed its own courses with internally moderated assessment.

While the impetus towards new courses—for example, CSE courses—and new learning approaches—for example, individualised learning—could have come from departments or senior management, it is the job of senior management to find resources of teachers, space, time, materials and equipment to implement the courses. The

---

*Readers outside Scotland should note that because transfer to secondary school occurs a year later than in England and Wales, class identifiers differ. S4 in Scotland is equivalent to S5 in England. The majority of pupils attain the age of 16 during that year. SCE stands for Scottish Certificate of Education. CSE is not a Scottish Examination but is nonetheless taken by pupils in some Scottish schools.

managements of Phase 2 schools seemed to have met the needs of teachers in providing those resources. Though discipline problems had certainly not disappeared from S3 and S4 classes in these schools, teachers and pupils alike had fewer complaints about courses and the pay off in terms of discipline was not lacking. Teachers reported that the introduction of CSE and like courses had been a major factor in decreasing discipline problems.

The Nature of Pupil-teacher Relationships

It must not be imagined that the schools which are abolishing or have abolished corporal punishment are identical in overall tone. Management sets the tone of a school. By countless decisions, through the ways senior management interacts with teachers and pupils, and through staff meetings where ideals are described, management can shape the quality of life in a school. The ideals of pupil-teacher relationships—an essential aspect of the tone of a school—can vary considerably, as was found in the research.

At one end of the spectrum was a "traditional" secondary school. Distance between pupils and teachers was maintained, especially between teachers and S1–S4 pupils. The senior management had successfully contrived to make school uniform compulsory. Many teachers and all the management team wore gowns; prefects and monitors performed duties, including enforcing the ban on pupils' using the building at intervals; vandalism and graffitti were visibly less than at many similar schools and an atmosphere of work and discipline pervaded the school. In contrast, another school allowed "students" (they were not called pupils) to use teachers' first names. No school uniform was worn and, indeed, older pupils and younger teachers were indistinguishable in dress anyway. As one student put it, the teachers "talk our way". The atmosphere would be described by some as relaxed, by others as lax. As a means to building the relationships between students and staff, each pupil was involved as part of the formal curriculum in a minimum of three field trips in the first three years of secondary schooling. The majority of staff took part in those trips. The belief held in this school was clearly that the control aspect of the teacher-pupil relationship can be achieved and exercised more inconspicuously than is the case with more conventional methods of social and classroom control. (See Appendix A for a brief description of a "relationships" model of discipline.)

In both these schools the head teachers seem to have been largely responsible for the establishment of the "ideals" or norms of pupil-teacher relationship. In the first case, the school was new and norms had had to be established. In the latter case the head teacher set about changing the norms which had been very different under the previous head teacher.

Conclusions

The part to be played by promoted staff—both within subject

departments and in the senior management team—in the discipline structure of a school has been observed to go well beyond backing up teachers. The management team and especially the head teacher set the tone of the school through formulating policy on a host of issues from school uniform to what constitutes the appropriate relationship between pupils and teachers. Through encouraging developments in curriculum, management teams in Phase 2 schools have, on the evidence of teachers, reduced the discipline problems arising out of inappropriate courses. Management of discipline may occur at departmental as well as central level: some schools indeed encourage departments to set their own codes of conduct within the overall discipline structure. School central management is, it seems, necessarily responsible for the organisation of referrals (routine and crisis) and of guidance. It is probably significant that in the course of the research the head teachers found, if they had not already done so, a need to distance themselves from the more routine discipline cases. The same point indeed could well arise for other senior staff, some of whom were much involved in routine discipline cases.

In all five Phase 2 schools, guidance staff and management both had a role in matters of discipline. The next chapter probes the nature of the involvement of guidance in discipline in those schools which had abolished or were abolishing corporal punishment.

CHAPTER 4

THE ROLE OF GUIDANCE IN
DISCIPLINE AND PUNISHMENT

The ideal of good guidance practice in Scottish secondary schools has emphasised the separateness of the guidance function from the punishment function. Generally, where instances of guidance teachers punishing children have been encountered, this has been judged as a deviation from the ideal. For instance, the research showed that, in a Phase 1 'control' school, two of the guidance staff were perceived by other teachers and pupils as the school "hatchet men". (One was a woman!) The two teachers and the headteacher stated that they would have preferred guidance not to have such an image. It is perhaps paradoxical that, in abolishing corporal punishment, the Phase 2 schools have, to different degrees, formally placed the guidance teacher in a role which is akin to a punishment role.

The Normal Guidance Role

The essence of this role has been the offering of support to pupils in such matters as course and career choices and personal and social problems. The guidance teacher has been a caring identifiable adult in what may otherwise be a large impersonal school. Punishment is normally incompatible with such a role. Perhaps the majority of schools are like two of the Phase 1 'control' schools which operated a referral system which went through the principal teacher (subject) rather than through guidance: the guidance staff could be called in but their contribution was likely to be to provide specific case knowledge, not to punish. Inherent in such a system is that disciplinary action, and in particular corporal punishment, may take place without guidance staff being involved at all.

Implications for Guidance of the Abolition of Corporal Punishment

The distinction between 'guidance' and 'punishment' becomes blurred when the punishment is not physical. The research indicated that the blurring probably occurs mainly as a result of the introduction of referral and reporting systems. These systems have been designed by managements to monitor general patterns of pupil behaviour and to help answer questions of how and why disciplinary difficulties arise with particular pupils. It is clearly inappropriate to leave guidance out of the referral and reporting systems since a substantial part of the work of guidance teachers is the accumulation of case knowledge relating to individual pupils.

The blurring of the distinction between guidance and punishment is increased further if the school decides that a child's parents should be approached about his behaviour. Increased parental involvement was found to be an integral part of the abolition process, and since parental involvement has traditionally involved guidance staff this further undermines the distinction between discipline and guidance.

Another implication for guidance operating in the non-corporal punishment system concerns the paper reports which were found to be a major feature of such systems. If guidance staff maintain a distance between themselves and daily disciplinary problems a great deal of information which would be useful to them may pass them by.

A central problem for guidance staff is clearly that becoming closely involved with such referral procedures, parental interviews, and so on may identify them to the children as disciplinary agents. However, some schools which seek to abolish corporal punishment do so as part of a general change in the nature of the relationship between teacher and child. In some sense this change is akin to developing a counselling, pastoral relationship between all teachers and children. In such settings the teacher involved with a child would expect to talk to him about his behaviour, speak to his parents if necessary, and in many ways operate as a guidance teacher would. Clearly this too, has implications for the official guidance system and a rationalisation must take place when such systems operate.

Caring versus Punishment

One school was found to have decisively rejected any attempt to reconcile the conflict experienced by guidance teachers in respect of their pastoral and disciplinary roles. In this school adverse reports do go directly to the guidance staff, who then decide the next course of action. This may involve rebuking the child, sending for his parents, issuing a behaviour timetable,* or passing on the referral further to the management team. While it was not the intention of this school to place the guidance staff in a position of disciplinary responsibility, they are inevitably perceived by the pupils as being so. In another Phase 2 school, guidance staff are allowed to counsel pupils, contact parents, give advice and feedback to subject teachers and, if necessary, refer the case on to the management team who may suspend, place in detention, or take whatever other action is deemed necessary. The role of the guidance staff here is much less obviously disciplinary and the school maintains the separation of guidance and discipline as a matter of policy. However it must be said that this distinction does not always appear to be a particularly real one. If guidance staff are the recipients of adverse reports and if, as a consequence, they see a child and speak to him about his behaviour and perhaps call in his parents then, whether they seek it

---

*For explanation of this term, see p 9.

or not, they are fulfilling a central disciplinary function. The fact that they pass the child on for detention or suspension may be meaningful to them but is less likely to be meaningful to the pupils. Further evidence of this tension between caring and punishing was found in the school which was new to the Phase 2 investigation. In this school, in the past guidance staff had involved themselves occasionally in belting pupils on behalf of other teachers but were now said to be attempting to stand back generally from a disciplinary role. They were not routinely contacted over disciplinary issues—where the referral line was from class teacher to principal teacher (subject)—and were called in only if the subject teachers felt that they had insufficient background information to deal with the problem themselves. However, they had clearly not shaken off their previous mantle completely. The five guidance staff interviewed reported putting 21 pupils on detention in one week and one guidance teacher in interview reported that he had suggested to some teachers that they did not use his name as a threat.

The two other Phase 2 schools represent contrasting approaches to dealing with the need to involve more teachers in "guidance" capacities while maintaining a distinct guidance team. In one case the approach involved demoting guidance from a central pastoral or disciplinary role. This was done firstly by having no AHT (guidance) and only two principal teachers of guidance. They were given purely functional remits, one for careers and the other for the school special unit. The remaining guidance staff, all assistant principals, were allocated in pairs to each "year head" to assist him generally in his duties. (They did not appear to have a distinctive guidance function and were not identified regularly by the pupils as the teacher they would approach if they had a problem.) The pastoral responsibility was laid upon the register teachers who were required by the relevant year head (AHT) to get to know their registration pupils. The distinction between caring and punishing had however largely been removed: the year head had total responsibility and would issue detention to a persistent troublemaker or befriend a timid child as the need arose.

In the other of the two schools the extension of guidance responsibility to a wider cross-section of teachers had been formalised by the creation of "guidance leaders". These were responsible for around twenty children each and were expected to get to know these children and to contact and interview their parents routinely. The official guidance system was responsible for giving support to these guidance leaders. Guidance in this school was held to have a diagnostic rather than a disciplinary function.

Conclusion

The abolition of corporal punishment produces a variety of problems for guidance. In particular, the distinction between pastoral care and discipline, which is perhaps not so very clear even in traditional settings, becomes more difficult to maintain. Also where, on account of the removal of corporal punishment, there is an alteration in the relationship between *all* teachers and pupils there are implications for guidance teachers. The Phase 2 schools sought to handle the problems in a variety of ways.

CHAPTER 5

MANAGING CHANGE

In examining those strategies that were used to abolish or diminish the use of corporal punishment, it is worth bearing in mind that those strategies may be quite different from those that would be employed should a general abolition take place. It is, nevertheless, likely that there will be lessons to be learned from an examination of the experiences of those teachers who have been involved in the process of abolition.

The Role of the Headteacher

It is a measure of the significance of the headteacher in the schools studied that in all cases, to a very great extent, the ethos of the school was a direct reflection of his personality and outlook. It was noticeable how much the *style* of the school reflected the headteacher. This, in itself, is a direct consequence of the *active* management approach of the various heads. To some extent they were constrained by their chosen aims to act in this way: since they had all decided to implement a discipline policy which was counter to current practices, they almost inevitably had to become active managers in order to achieve it. (However, there was also evidence in the extent of curricular developments to suggest that all the headteachers of Phase 2 schools were active in promoting change in a wider sphere than discipline.)

In four of the Phase 2 schools the first action of the headteacher, on appointment, seems to have been to make a clear statement of his personal opposition to the use of corporal punishment. In the fifth school, the headteacher, though less committed to total abolition, made known his wish to reduce the incidence of corporal punishment. While several of the heads had certainly been users of corporal punishment in previous schools, there were no instances of a head declaring a *change* in his attitude to corporal punishment while in any of the schools studied. In short, all of the heads studied were consistent in their position on corporal punishment while in that school. Of course, this is likely to be quite counter to what may be the position of heads in other schools should general abolition take place. Such heads would have to change their behaviour and policy, if not their attitude. This change may make for difficulty since it was very clear that the impact and persuasiveness of the head's position, while always strong, was made more so by its consistency. (These remarks apply more insistently if we are referring to a general and voluntary abolition. Presumably if abolition is imposed heads have no need to justify to their staffs a change of attitude.)

In keeping with much of the above, there were no examples in the schools studied of a head being strongly influenced towards abolition by a committed staff group. In two of the schools there was a staff vote taken prior to the implementation of policy. However, in both cases there were good reasons for the headteachers to believe that a majority of the staff would support abolition. One vote was taken in a new school prior to opening. The school had almost certainly attracted a largely self-selected staff group who would be more likely to favour abolition. In the other vote-taking school, the vote was taken after the head had been in post for seven years. During this period belting had been progressively reduced and the school had acquired a certain reputation for non-traditional innovations. The reputation certainly attracted sympathetic staff and the head's selection criterion may have helped further in producing a staff sympathetic to abolition. It should also be noted that in both schools the headteacher's position was made quite clear prior to the voting. In the three other schools, where there was perhaps at first a more representative spectrum of teacher views, no vote was ever taken and the decision to make the move towards abolition was essentially the head's. There were commonly extensive consultations with staff and the method and time-scale of introduction varied—these will be considered in the following sections—but broadly speaking abolition, or moves in the philosophy of discipline in the direction of abolition, were imposed.

There were no major differences of view within the management teams in any of the schools. Consistency of views would not be surprising in those cases where the appointments were made following the arrival of the heads. However, in several instances, this was not the case and the heads had "inherited" promoted staff. There were no observed instances of disaffected senior management holding pro-corporal punishment views. This may be, in part at least, sheer pragmatism on the part of such teachers. Alternatively, the heads may have persuaded their management colleagues. It may also be that fiercely opposed members had left the schools earlier.

Time-Scale

Not surprisingly there was no standard time-scale or procedure for the abolition process in the schools studied. There was, however, a degree of uniformity in what was not attempted. No head appointed to an existing school abolished corporal punishment immediately upon taking up his post. Only one school had never used the belt and that was a new community school. The facts of a new school, a committed headmaster, a community ethos, and a selected staff group would suggest that this was not a generalisable experience. Notice, however, that the vast majority of teachers came from traditional Scottish schools, as they did in the other new school. In this second new school the head did not ever ban the use of the belt. To use the headteacher's own words, "It just fell into disuse". He actively discouraged its use from the beginning, established a recording system for *all* punishments including the belt, and set up a comprehensive discipline package as if the belt was not used. This led to total disuse of corporal punishment after two years, by which time the non-use of corporal punishment became a reified part of the school policy. (It seems that in the second year of operation the belt was used on only four occasions.)

The three schools that remain were all existing schools with a change of headteacher. The two schools situated in Strathclyde made use of the Region's Standard Circular 21* in progressing towards abolition. In one of the Strathclyde schools, after two years in post during which time he did not belt, the head implemented SC21 "to the letter" for three years. Thereafter, the belt was totally banned in S1, S5 and S6 and the next year the "experiment" continued with S2 added.§ The position in June 1981 was that only boys in S3 and S4 could be belted and then only by male staff. There was every indication that belting had largely ended in this school. It was planned to extend the ban on corporal punishment progressively over the next two years until it applied to all classes.

In the second Strathclyde school, SC21 was taken up by the head immediately upon appointment. However, despite a reduction in belting as a result of the adoption of SC21 and other measures—including a reporting and referral system—no further steps had been taken up to June 1981 and it appeared that a small residue of teachers were continuing to use corporal punishment. The head teacher's strategy amounted to providing an alternative system of sanctions to operate alongside, or in combination with, corporal punishment, and to encouraging the use of the former and the reduction of the latter, so as to let teachers choose individually when to discontinue using corporal punishment. It appeared that he did not wish to ban corporal punishment until it had virtually disappeared.

In the third school a committed head appointed to a traditional school took seven years to remove the belt completely. During this period he refused to belt, stated his opposition, made changes in the school's approach to discipline designed to reduce the incidence of belting, and asked staff to continue to log its use after an Education Authority initiative had temporarily required schools to keep a log. This approach, plus staff changes, resulted in a majority staff vote in favour of total abolition at the end of the seven year period.

Consultation

The interviews and discussions with the management teams, and more particularly the heads in the sampled schools, revealed a considerable emphasis on extensive consultations with staff *before* implementing policy changes of all kinds. However, consultation tended to be over tactics rather than strategy. As indicated, the tendency

---

*The circular enshrines the 1968 Code of Practice on Corporal Punishment.

§The pupils in S2 had, of course, already been in a non-corporal punishment environment in S1 in the previous year.

was for the corporal punishment innovation to be largely the province of the headteacher. The new disciplinary systems were flexible enough to respond and did respond to suggestions and complaints by individual staff members. Indeed, such responsiveness was felt to be imperative for the systems to function. There is, therefore, a paradox inherent in this area. On the one hand, we have pictures of very committed and powerful heads and Boards of Studies and, on the other, declared policies of openness and potential responsiveness to teachers' anxieties and problems. Not surprisingly, such a paradox was often perceived by teachers in the schools. Many remarked that the head and management team *were* accepting and accessible, but had usually made up their minds already. Nevertheless, teacher interviews did indicate that in two areas in particular these schools were strong. First, the management teams were generally approachable and ready to listen to staff. There were, for example, remarkably few references by staff to feelings of being assessed adversely as a result of referring on discipline problems. Second, downward communication from management was generally very efficient in the schools studied. Staff were made well aware of the various aspects of the discipline policy. There were, surprisingly, teachers in every Phase 2 school ignorant of some elements of the system, but extremely few. (Evidence from Phase 1 schools suggests that complete communication of discipline policy does not always occur and that, in some schools, teachers feel changes happen without satisfactory teacher involvement.)

Publicity

Whether to give much, little, or no publicity to the abolition of corporal punishment was a matter on which the heads of the Phase 2 schools differed. Some feared that publicity would jeopardise their chances of success and give rise to indiscipline. One school that at the time of the investigation was still in the course of abolition gave no publicity at all. Another school, before embarking on progressive abolition, limited publicity to a mention, embedded in a letter to the parents of pupils entering first year, that there would be no corporal punishment for their children. In contrast, one school deliberately sought publicity through national media. In the event, the reactions to publicity—low, medium or high—seem to have been very small. Nonetheless those who sought to keep publicity low appear to have retained their view that caution is desirable.

Summary

All the schools which have abolished corporal punishment or reduced the levels of corporal punishment approached the change differently. However, in each case the move was largely on the initiative of the headteacher and, though the time-scale differed, no headteacher abolished corporal punishment immediately upon appointment to an existing school. A summary of the salient features of each Phase 2 school (including the changes introduced) is contained in Appendix B).

D

CHAPTER 6

TEACHER ATTITUDES TO THE ABOLITION OF CORPORAL PUNISHMENT

Three positions on the question of abolition of corporal punishment showed up amongst the teachers interviewed.

1 Those who favoured retention.
2 Those who favoured a gradual phasing out, and saw the strap as useful until other sanctions were identified.
3 Those who wanted to abolish it immediately or very quickly.

The primary concerns of teachers who support retention of corporal punishment focussed on the questions of immediacy and on a possible deterioration in the pupils' standards of behaviour:

"Punishment must be there as retribution and deterrent."

Principal Teacher, Phase 1, retentionist school.

"I cannot see how discipline can be enforced without it. There is nothing to take its place."

Teacher, Phase 1, control school.

The issue of immediacy is linked to the view that punishment, if associated quickly, publicly, and clearly with an offence, combines a retributive and a deterrent aspect. Teachers in the schools where corporal punishment was abolished or being abolished did on occasion make reference to the time taken by alternatives. Some of them clearly missed the immediacy of the strap:

"I'd like to see corporal punishment go: but, effective *immediate* sanctions are needed. Other sanctions take too long. Detention takes days."

Teacher, Phase 1, abolitionist school.

As a consequence of the lack of immediacy, teachers who favoured retention feared that poorer pupil behaviour would result.

Those teachers who favoured abolition of corporal punishment held that corporal punishment is no good for really difficult aggressive pupils, that it prevents good teacher-pupil relationships, and that it treats only the symptoms, not the causes, of bad behaviour.

Comparison of Teacher Attitudes in Phases 1 and 2

A proportion of teachers in four schools were interviewed in both Phases 1 and 2. The significant findings were that no teacher who in Phase 1 supported abolition now wished to use corporal punishment but that, on the other hand, a few teachers had changed from wishing that their school would retain corporal punishment to accepting that it functioned happily without it:

Phase 1: "I am opposed to abolition. I cannot accept abolition without a proven practical working alternative . . . even then not certain . . . Anyway, I haven't heard of one."
Principal Teacher in school abolishing Corporal Punishment.

Phase 2: "I am not opposed to seeing it (corporal punishment) go. Referral works and achieves some success."

Same teacher.

Almost invariably, even those teachers who by Phase 2 still believed it preferable to have corporal punishment retained shared their colleagues' positive conviction that their school's new discipline system was a success—a conviction that was tempered by an awareness of weak points yet to be overcome. Comments of teachers interviewed in Phase 2 (ie one year after Phase 1) showed a shift in emphasis from discipline policy—the principle of abolition—to discipline procedures—immediacy, feedback and tolerance levels. There was an awareness that the immediacy of punishment associated with the strap was just not applicable to other available sanctions. Positive efforts were being made to give teachers adequate feedback. The impression left on the issue was that the point would soon be reached where any dissatisfaction about the level of feedback would be more likely to be due to the failures of individuals than to the system itself.

To sum up, the teachers in the thirteen schools investigated were divided, even polarised, in their attitudes to the abolition of the strap. When the views of those teachers in schools where abolition had occurred or was occurring are considered, two points can be made. First, the research came across no example of teachers who changed camp from the abolitionists to the retentionists. Second, generally by Phase 2 teachers accepted abolition in principle but were concerned about the procedures used in connection with the various other sanctions.

The picture to be drawn from the schools which have abolished the strap or are well on the way to doing so is of teachers who are, by and large, coping well with discipline without using the strap.

What outsiders would like to know, of course, is whether standards of pupil behaviour in those schools have dropped. Are there riots in the classrooms? Do police have to be called in regularly to keep the peace?

Straightaway we can dismiss fears that chaos reigns in the non-belting schools. To the various teams of researchers there were no signs of impending chaos in any school. The degrees of control exercised by the teachers in classrooms were observed to be very similar to those exercised in schools which retained the strap. In general, teachers reported that their pupils were at least as well behaved and interested in learning as in similar schools. Many, however, did recognise that some minor incidents were not punished: their "tolerance of trifling incidents tended to increase" in the absence of resort to the strap. It was widely held that the increased tolerance was balanced by a more relaxed relationship between pupils and teachers. Much antagonism and many 'them and us' attitudes had disappeared with the belt.

The final words on teacher attitudes to the use of corporal punishment are those of a teacher interviewed in Phase 1 in a school where abolition had recently arrived:

> "Now I know my teaching is as effective as it was previously. There's no barrier between teachers and pupils as before."
>
> *Teacher, 14 years' teaching experience.*

CHAPTER 7

MESSAGES . . .

1 To Education Authorities

1 Belting is an inexpensive sanction.

2 There is no one single "alternative" sanction.

3 The schools which operated completely without corporal punishment and those which were eliminating corporal punishment all had what may be called 'standing plans' for discipline. Major elements within these plans were formal guidance systems (which, through counselling, tried to establish the root causes of indiscipline), special units (in which a small number of potentially disruptive pupils were given more personal educational programmes), and, in some cases, forms of detention.

4 The guidance systems and the special units demand staffing which is *either* additional to the school establishment *or* is re-allocated to these jobs from other tasks. In short, this staffing has a cost either to the Authority or to the school.

5 The investigation showed that it took the schools a substantial time to plan and introduce alternative sanctions. (Only one school—which was not just a new school but a radical departure from traditional models of a secondary—had never used corporal punishment at all.) In one school, abolition did not take place until the head had been in office seven years, in another school (a new one) until the third session of its existence. In the other two schools, abolition had been introduced slowly for five sessions and three sessions respectively. While there may be telescoping of the phases of abolition if an Authority decides on a general abolitionist policy, there are no grounds in this research for supposing that instant abolition will be successful.

6 Authorities may find it advantageous to arrange specialist consultancy services for schools which wish to design appropriate referral and reporting systems. (See Chapter 2).

7 The question of the confidentiality and length of life of school records of children's behaviour is bound to concern parents. Authorities may wish to lay down guidelines for schools on (i) the access to behaviour record files; (ii) the security of their files; (iii) the use of behaviour record files in references to prospective employers and further education establishments. Since any honest and useful

reference to a prospective employer must take at least some account of how a pupil has behaved in school, it may in practice be impossible to establish whether any particular reference has been based on records or merely on the recollections of staff (as has long been the practice). Any decision by an Authority to ban the use of records for the purpose of job references might well therefore be ineffective save in stopping teachers using the threat of using records for that purpose as a means of influencing pupil behaviour in school. It is at least arguable that pupils should be brought to realise that persistent misconduct in school may operate to their own disadvantage after leaving school; and no less that, where a pupil has reformed, earlier misdemeanours should be disregarded in any reference.

8   Some Authorities already have codes covering procedures towards suspension and expulsion. It has been found that in trying to increase the perceived severity of formal suspension, the schools have invented two weaker unofficial types of suspension viz: "sent home for clarification" and "tactical/overnight suspension". Authorities will wish to consider whether schools using these unofficial forms of suspension merit official approval and support.

2 To Parents

1   At present only a tiny proportion of parents are likely to be invited to visit their child's school on account of his behaviour, even though they may well do so to discuss choice of courses or for social occasions. In all schools where the strap has been phased out or has been in the process of being phased out, a much larger proportion of parents have been involved, in one way or another, with the school over their children's behaviour.

2   The need to contact parents may arise from
    (a) the need of guidance staff to understand the reasons for recurrent misdemeanours—which may be curricular, social, emotional etc. (Sometimes contact by telephone may be sufficient to yield the necessary information, eg about some new home circumstance which has disturbed the pupil.)
    (b) to seek parental assistance in dealing with grave misconduct such as a fight or vandalism, or with persistent though less serious misconduct. (In this case parents, pupil and teachers need to work together to try to work out some way of bringing the pupil to behave acceptability, and indeed in serious cases parents may need to be invited to sign a guarantee of their child's good behaviour in the future.)

3   It is clear that the likelihood of parental involvement in a school discipline matter is not at all welcome by the vast majority of pupils,

and that the threat of informing their parents is likely to deter many from indiscipline.

3 To Headteachers

1 The key figure in all the case studies of abolition was the headteacher. Not only did the idea apparently spring from him but, in all cases, the headteacher carried his senior management colleagues with him and together they formed a united team which managed the innovation skilfully.

2 The headteacher who decides to move towards abolition has two main tasks. First, he has to decide *how* he is going to implement the change. Second, he has to decide *which* sanctions he will employ in the place of corporal punishment, *what* referral/reporting systems he will develop, and *what* measures he will introduce to reduce the incidence of misbehaviour.

3 All the headteachers who effected, or were effecting, the abolition of corporal punishment found it essential to consult extensively with their staffs. Indeed, one of them stated:

> "I would hate to try to do away with corporal punishment without being in a school where there was a lot of consultation about policy generally."

It would be fair to say that headteachers of the Phase 2 schools put their efforts (1) into having their aim of abolition accepted by their senior colleagues, (2) into communicating their intentions to other staff, and (3) into having teachers participate in the forming of the procedures by which the entire discipline system was to be operated. One headteacher produced a starter paper of some 17 pages setting the scene for departmental and inter-departmental discussions. Another headteacher arranged for eight *ad-hoc* groups of teachers to discuss the plan for abolition with the depute head. In two schools full staff debates were held and votes taken. Whatever the arrangements that were made to involve staff in the plans for abolition, once the change was underway staff comments and evaluations resulted in important minor changes to the operation of sanctions—eg to devise means for systematically following up detention defaulters—and to the referral and reporting systems—eg to formalise the feedback to class teachers on action taken. In short, while the policy, once dopted, may not change, the procedures for effecting it have to be flexible. It is likely that staff confidence in the changes will develop as they see their complaints answered and their suggestions implemented.

4 Reporting and information transmission—key aspects of policy in most of the 'abolition' schools—depend on well designed and efficiently operated clerical systems. Such systems will *not* be

efficiently operated unless teachers are clearly informed about both what the procedures are and what their aims are. (Early criticism of new discipline systems in the 'abolition' schools had more to do with the mechanics of operation than with the disciplinary system in principle).

5   Although time and care invested in the design of the forms, in the flow of information to and from guidance, management, and class teachers, and in the storage and summarising of collected information seems essential, a discipline system is not an efficient paper chase. Referrals must result in *action* by those responsible.

6   Headteachers can avoid some early misunderstanding among teachers by clarifying the distinction between reports (giving or sharing of information) and referrals (partly information about a failure to control a pupil's behaviour but also partly a request for help from upper levels in the referral chain). Teachers may not need or desire feedback on a report: they certainly will expect to know officially what has happened to a pupil referred upwards.

7   Teachers will report and refer as often as is desirable only if it is made manifest to them that their status and career prospects will be affected in no way by their revealing that cases of indiscipline have occurred in their classrooms.

8   Decisions to be taken as part of the reporting/referral system include
    (i)   the role to be played by guidance teachers;
    (ii)   the relationship of guidance staff to senior management staff, including the question of how distant the headteacher should be from routine discipline. (See Chapter 4);
    (iii) whether departmental heads should filter reports and referrals coming from class teachers;
    (iv)   at what stage parents should be informed and by whom;
    (v)   whether pupils should be threatened with reports or with guidance teachers;
    (vi)   whether pupils should be led to believe that reports on behaviour could be used against them with, say, prospective employers;
    (vii) whether files of behaviour records should be retained beyond a single school session.
    (viii) how to deal with the small number of teachers or departments who either overuse the system or ignore it altogether.

9   Headteachers have to work out their graduated sanctions list (cf Table 1, p 6). There seem to be two principles to be drawn from practice. First, a sanction is as severe as it is made to seem. Second, over-use of any sanction reduces its deterrent value. For instance, the sanction of detention surrounded by a rigmarole of procedure

and supervised by a senior promoted teacher is a more severe sanction than a detention of the same length in the class where the offence was committed. The school-supervised detention must not be over-used, or else its perceived severity collapses.

10   If the school is to use detention as a penalty at times when pupils would normally be returning home, it is essential that parents be informed in advance. Indeed it is probably necessary for their written consent to the detention to be obtained if difficulties over the legality of the detention are to be avoided. It needs also to be remembered that lunch-time detention may well make it necessary for the pupil to bring a packed lunch. For all these reasons, detention of a pupil on the same day as the penalty is imposed is, save in unusual circumstances, out of the question.

11   Where pupils travel considerable distances to school—and especially where they use special school buses—detention is probably practicable only at lunch-time.

4   To Teachers

1   Quite simply no discipline structure, however carefully devised and skilfully introduced, will function without the cooperation of the class teacher. The research indicated that the profession was divided, even polarised, over the question of abolition of the strap. Hence, strongly held views against abolition are bound to exist in perhaps a majority of schools. If it is any comfort to those with such views, there were, in the abolitionist schools, teachers who felt at the outset very sceptical of the whole notion of abolition and who were yet convinced after one or two sessions of working the new system, that *their* school was able to manage without the strap. (Teachers were more cautious about generalising to all schools the apparent success of their own school's "experiment").

2   A discipline system without corporal punishment is one in which individual teachers are more open about the difficulties they have with pupils. They share with others—perhaps their departmental head, perhaps with guidance teachers and even senior management—information about patterns of behaviour. Passing on information is not always, or even commonly, an admission of failure with a particular pupil. It is just as likely to be a report that, for instance, a pupil, previously in trouble, has suddenly become openly inattentive and has been given some punishment. This information will be collated with information from other parts of the school and thus a pupil's behaviour throughout the school will be monitored. At some later date guidance or senior management may feed back to the reporting teacher their assessment of the

41

pupil's problem and, perhaps, give advice on dealing with him when difficulties occur.

3   The pay-off for teachers who actively cooperate in a behaviour assessment scheme such as that sketched above may be a marked reduction in feelings of being isolated, of being the only one with problems with a particular class or pupil. Moreover, the solution to the pupil with behaviour problems may be slower in coming than a quick belting but it will be a solution which works more effectively in the long term. For instance, parents may be enlisted to guarantee the good behaviour of a child. In short, solutions which take time may be solutions to problems, not symptoms.

4   Some teachers may regard regular referrals or reports of pupils' behaviour as a reflection of their professional competence. Since openness of reporting and referring would appear to be a prerequisite of a usable behaviour assessment system, it is important that teachers recognise that the concept of teacher professionalism is extendable. Thus, whereas a 'good' teacher may have been, in the past, one who handled and kept problems within his classroom, the extended concept of professionalism implied in the school-wide behaviour assessment system is of the teacher who shares knowledge and problems with colleagues in order to find the best solution for the child. Management have a task initially in assuring all teachers that no dossiers consolidating reports by individual teachers will be kept, far less used.

5   Teachers know themselves that even within a single department there are those who are stricter and those who are fussier than others. The research showed that in the upper levels of referral chains decisions were taken to take less serious note of some reports ('pencil forgotten') than others ('rampaging in the library'). It is inevitable that some filtering of reports will be done at the upper levels. The amount of necessary filtering can be minimised by teachers and management (1) discussing acceptable and unacceptable behaviour in classrooms, (2) agreeing on the supervision of, and responsibility for, behaviour in corridors, stairs, playground, (3) formulating and operating a graduated list of sanctions.

APPENDIX A

A RELATIONSHIPS MODEL OF DISCIPLINE

The features of such a "relationships" model of discipline were observed in School D (see Appendix B) which gave the name to model. However, there were signs that School X was also moving towards the model.

The key to the relationships model lies in the espoused aim of the school viz, to build positive relationships between teachers and pupils (or students, as this school prefers to call them). An act of indiscipline *may* lead to a breaking of that relationship. If that happens, trust has to be restored. It is as a consequence of the adoption of the model that there are no specific school rules as such. Rules are, therefore, not broken: relationships may be. Students have to work at restoring the relationships rather than suffer punishment for breaking a rule.

Great stress is put on staff and students 'negotiating' when a relationship has broken down. The talking out process is clearly extremely time-consuming for the set of expectations of pupil behaviour in the school are not materially different from those held by staffs of other schools in the survey. To assist in the maintenance of relationships, sanctions are employed. Moreover, guidance is regarded as a positive aid to establishing relationships in the school. Each student is one of a group of 20 which, in principle, has the same guidance leader for the entire period of compulsory secondary level schooling. The guidance leader sees his group for 30 minutes each morning (and sometimes also as a subject teacher). Most teachers are guidance leaders. Guidance leaders are supported by promoted guidance teachers whose teaching load enable them to spend time on counselling. Fortnightly guidance case-conferences are held which all involved are invited to attend in order to contribute to a review of individual student's cases. The case conferences and the one-to-one counselling are essentially diagnostic and aim to understand a student's behaviour, then to halt and reverse a decline in acceptable behaviour.

FEATURES OF PHASE 2 SCHOOLS—THOSE WHICH HAD ABOLISHED OR WERE ABOLISHING CORPORAL PUNISHMENT (1980/81)

	SCHOOL A	SCHOOL B	SCHOOL C	SCHOOL D	SCHOOL X
Period(s) Visited	Phase 1—Feb. 1980 Phase 2—Feb. 1981	Phase 1—March 1980 Phase 2—Feb. 1981	Phase 1—Mid May-Mid June 1980 Phase 2—February, March 1981	Phase 1—May-June 1980 Phase 2—March 1981	Not included in Phase 1 Phase 2—March 1981
Roll	Approximately 1600	Approximately 1150	Approximately 1100	Approximately 1300	Approximately 1100
Management Structure	Head, Depute, and 5 AHTs, one of whom has guidance responsibilities; others have whole school responsibilities but with allotted tasks.	Head, 2 Deputes, 1 AHT Lower School, 1 AHT Middle 1 AHT Upper 1 AHT Functional	Head, Depute and 4 AHTs. Each Depute and AHT has total responsiblity for a year group.	Head, Depute and 6 AHTs of whom 3 are "mini-heads" of Lower, Middle and Upper Schools.	Head, Depute and 5 AHTs, all functional; one has guidance responsibilities.
Guidance Structure	Horizontal: each year group has its guidance staff. PT (Guidance) usually with his/her group from S1–S6.	Horizontal: guidance teams (PT with 1 or more APT) are static within Lower, Middle and Upper Schools.	Horizontal: 2 PTs (Guidance) and AHT and DHT per year group. 2 PTs Guidance have functional remits.	Horizontal: each pupil is in a guidance group under a guidance leader who is supported by a PT or APT (Guidance). Guidance teachers are static within Lower, Middle and Upper schools.	Vertical, based on 3 houses; 2 PT and 1 APT (Guidance) for each House.
Age of School	About 8 years old	About 10 years old	Opened in 1977	Opened in 1978	More than 10 years old
Catchment Area	Serves 3 small towns with history of inter-town rivalry. Mixed housing, about 60% council-owned, 30% private and 10%	Semi-industrial urban community with small numbers of rural children. Part of area is designated as multiply deprived	A good social mix. 4 council estates and 1 private estate.	100% council housing of post-war type. Many one-parent families.	100% council housing By all indicators, it is multiply deprived.

Detention	School organised official detention at lunch-time, supervised by senior staff. Parents informed in advance. There is also some class teacher detention.	No detention	Some departmental detention but decreasing in favour of post-school official detention supervised by rota of senior and volunteer staff. Parents informed in advance.	Detention is increasingly on a departmental rather than class teacher basis. Parents informed in advance by letter Length of detention varies up to one hour No school-organised detention.	Detention on a departmental and class teacher basis. Increasing formalisation of procedure e.g. names of detainees written in Detention Logs kept in staff room. No school-organised detention.
Isolation	Not operated	Not formalised but some use made of administration area where supervision is by senior staff.	Punishment unit is a special kind of isolation for an extended period (up to 3 weeks); a PT (Guidance) runs the unit.	"Time-out". Ready cooperation between staff of the same dept. allows trouble-some pupils to be moved to another group or area, with work.	"On-Assignment" Formalised in a pro-forma. Widely used by teachers who can "arrange" beforehand with colleagues to accept a pupil "on assignment.
Withdrawal of Privilege	Not prominent	Not prominent	Privileges which can be withdrawn include attendance at disco sessions, outings within the curriculum school trips and membership of school clubs.	Right of access to community facilities can be withdrawn.	Not prominent
"On Report" (Behaviour Timetable)	Not operated	Some use of behaviour timetables	Use made of behaviour timetables	Not operated	Not operated
Suspension	Follows Regional Policy in using only formal suspension.	Follows Regional Policy in using only formal suspension; its use automatic for vandalism.	Includes two stages prior to official suspension. These are "being sent home for clarification" and "tactical suspension".	Suspension is not stressed in the discipline policy, which is based on a relationships model. (See Appendix A)	Suspension, in an unofficial form, is automatic for fighting. Otherwise it follows Regional Policy.

(continued overleaf)

45

	SCHOOL A	SCHOOL B	SCHOOL C	SCHOOL D	SCHOOL X
Reporting and Referral Systems	Report form passes from class teacher, through departmental head, to the relevant PT (Guidance) for evaluation/ initial non-punitive action. After 3 reports an AHT is advised and acts. Feedback is given to the referring teacher.	A report form is completed by a class teacher and forwarded-through the departmental head, who completes a section on departmental action, to the guidance team who evaluate and act. If appropriate, a feedback pro forma is completed by guidance for the referring teacher.	Separate report and referral forms are the basis of the discipline system (see Chapter 2). Discipline surveys also contribute to spotting potential trouble-makers. Feedback to teachers comes from the results of the periodic discipline surveys and, when appropriate, from the year teams.	A discipline referral form is expected to be completed by teachers. The system is less integral to the non-corporal punishment policy than in Schools A, B and C. There is an upwards referral process for crisis and discipline refusal cases.	A discipline letter exists for completion by principal teachers in the cases of pupils with discipline problems they cannot resolve. For "crisis" referrals there is an "on call" list of two staff for each period.
Involvement of guidance in discipline.	Guidance used in the first stages of evaluating teacher reports. The *aim* is to keep guidance out of punishment.	Guidance evaluate and act on reports. They can rebuke, call in parents etc. Being placed in the referral chain between referring teacher (and his PT) and senior staff they have a disciplinary role.	Traditional guidance teacher does not exist. Pastoral and discipline roles combined in year-head, who, for years 1–4, is an AHT, and, for years 5/6, the Depute.	Guidance has a diagnostic rather than disciplinary role. Staff recognise the distinction. The various AHTs have a more direct discipline role than guidance staff	Guidance staff are involved in discipling as points of reference in the Houses, both for information and as punishers, e.g. by imposing detention.
Role of Management in Discipline.	Management staff involved at second stage when a significant number of reports has accumulated on a pupil. There is some distancing of management from early stages of referral and reporting.	Management staff are the top of the guidance teams, which both monitor reports and act.	The AHT's and Depute are more closely associated with discipline in their roles of "mini-heads" and because the traditional concept of guidance is combined with the "mini-head" role. Depute maintains the key role in crisis	Senior management may play a harsher role vis à vis guidance but are distant from the early stages as guidance diagnoses problems. Management play a support role to designated departments in a crisis	Management are distant from all stages of referral except in a crisis referral, when they are "on call". They are involved in following-up those who default on detention.

Discipline.	courses. (ii) Link courses with FE (iii) Block timetable	and less easily motivated S3 and S4 pupils. (ii) Some individualised learning in S1 and S2 subjects. (iii) Block timetable.	able S3/S4 pupils. School's own certificate is internally moderated.	(ii) Foundation level City and Guild's courses. (iii) Half year course in practical subjects and work experience for S4.	approximately 40% of S3/S4.
Special Unit	Sanctuary type unit in a flat situated 1/4 mile from school. Unit staffing is full-time. Some pupils maintain partial links with main school. Reintegration is not common.	Sanctuary type unit in a separate transportable unit. Unit staffing is full-time but there is some involvement of teachers from main school. Reintegration is less than school would like.	Punishment type unit. PT (guidance) in charge; staffing by good disciplinarians, atmosphere of regimentation. Reintegration follows after 2–3 weeks.	Sanctuary type unit in a formerly unused space. Teachers from main school are involved though most teaching by 3 part-time teachers. Reintegration is slow.	Sanctuary type unit in remote part of school. Formal assessment of pupil at entry. Two teachers do most of the teaching. Reintegration only partly successful: some part-time pupils in attendance.
How abolition was achieved or is being achieved.	Step 1 Logging of corporal punishment begun in 1973/74; courses adopted to cater for less able in S3/S4. Step 2 Decline of recorded use of the strap to 5% of its 1973–4 level by 1979–80. Step 3 Vote of staff on abolition in August 1980: majority in favour. *Abolition complete.*	Step 1 Vote of staff on abolition prior to opening in 1978. Majority in favour. Relationships Model of discipline adopted. Step 2 Vote of staff on retaining abolition in 1979: unanimous in favour. *No use of corporal punishment in this school ever.*	Step 1 New school in 1977. Staff encouraged not to use strap. Behaviour assessment system implemented as part of package to replace strap. Step 2 By 1979–80 no use of strap. *Abolition complete.* Step 3 In 1980–81 school organised detention replacing other weaker forms of detention.	Step 1 Gradual enforcement of 1968 code of practice on corporal punishment over 1978–1980. Step 2 Design of report/referral system in 1979–80. Step 3 Modification of report/referral system to include provision for feedback to teachers in 1980–81. *Corporal punishment not yet banned but use at minimal level.*	Step 1 Enforced 1968 "code of practice" on corporal punishment. Step 2 Strap abolished for S1 and S5 and S6 in '79–80. Step 3 Strap abolished for S2 in '80–81 Before Step 2, consultation was extensive. Abolition for S1 was viewed as experimental. Report system was modified during Step 2. *Abolition will be complete by August 1982.*

APPENDIX C

TYPICAL REPORTING AND FEEDBACK FORMS

FORM A (REFERRAL FOR ACTION)

Pupil	*Class*	*Report*
	Principal Teacher	

FORM B (INFORMATION)

Pupil	*Class and Subject*	*Report*
	Teacher	

FORM C (REPORT BACK*)

NAME	Class

The above pupil received an adverse comment from you a few weeks ago. I would be grateful for a note of any change or improvement.

Subject	*Comment*

*In effect, a request for further information from the teacher.

48